The Little Book of
# Colouring for Mindfulness

An Hachette UK Company
www.hachette.co.uk
First published in Great Britain in 2016 by
ILEX, a division of Octopus Publishing Group Ltd
Octopus Publishing Group
Carmelite House
50 Victoria Embankment
London, EC4Y 0DZ
www.octopusbooks.co.uk
www.octopusbooksusa.com

Distributed in the US by
Hachette Book Group
1290 Avenue of the Americas
4th and 5th Floors
New York, NY 10104

Distributed in Canada by
Canadian Manda Group
664 Annette St.
Toronto, Ontario, Canada M6S 2C8

The mandalas in this book have previously been published in
*Flower Mandalas* and *Nature Mandalas to Colour for Calm*

PUBLISHER: Roly Allen
COMMISSIONING EDITOR: Zara Larcombe
MANAGING EDITOR: Frank Gallaugher
SENIOR PROJECT EDITOR: Natalia Price-Cabrera
EDITOR: Rachel Silverlight
ART DIRECTOR: Julie Weir
DESIGN: Made Noise
PRODUCTION CONTROLLER: Sarah Kulasek-Boyd

ISBN 978-1-78157-388-4

A CIP catalogue record for this book is available
from the British Library

Printed and bound in Europe

10 9 8 7 6 5

# The Little Book of
# **Colouring for Mindfulness**

## 100 Mandalas for Instant Calm

**Cynthia Emerlye**

## WHAT IS A MANDALA?

For thousands of years people have considered the circle to be symbolic of wholeness, oneness, eternity and the Cosmos. A circle has no breaking point, no inception and no terminus; you can trace a circle with your finger and never come to the end of it. In the same way, mandalas, which are often circular in shape, use repeating patterns to suggest the continuous and cyclical nature of life. Mandalas are one of the oldest art forms intended to represent a spiritual idea, and they can be found in every culture.

## HOW DO MANDALAS WORK?

The repetitive nature of these designs helps focus and calm the mind; instead of trying to compose, arrange or think through a maze, one simply has to follow a design around and around, noticing the intricacies of its repetition. The repetition of simple motifs within a circle creates patterns more complex and interesting than the elements themselves, and focusing one's attention on these patterns can have the dual effect of both calming the nerves and stimulating attention. Simply looking at a complex mandala can have this effect.

## COLOURING TO DE-STRESS

Going further and colouring in the design deepens and prolongs these benefits. It's no wonder that colouring mandalas has become a favourite way to relax in this hectic world, and this book is designed to go anywhere with you, offering you a chance to unwind wherever you are—even if you have only a few spare minutes.

## NATURAL MANDALAS

The hundred mandalas in this book all
draw upon themes from the natural world.
You will find flowers, plant life, birds, insects,
mammals, reptiles and creatures of all sorts
cleverly wound into the designs. Leaves,
flowers and vines connect them into an
elegant tapestry of flora and fauna shapes.
Apart from evoking the beauties of nature,
these designs are deliberately complex,
inviting you to slow down and pay attention.
Take your time colouring, and allow yourself
to focus inward: breathe, relax and enjoy.

## COLOURING IN

There is no right or wrong way to colour these designs—so you can set aside any anxiety you may have about your artistic ability, and relax into the simple pleasure of laying down colour. Because of the complexity of the designs, you will need fine-tipped instruments such as coloured pencils, gel pens and fine or brush-tipped markers. Staying inside the lines will improve the final result. Make each motif stand out by placing darker colours next to light ones.

## CREATIVE COLOUR

Experimenting with colour combinations on a piece of scrap paper before you put them on your mandala can help avoid regrettable choices. Otherwise, have fun! Experiment with the unusual if you feel adventurous; make a horse blue and a flower green if you so desire. If you are feeling subdued, a quiet palette might feel right – or you can liven things up with bright, cheerful colours. Try using shades of the same colour throughout, or colour in the negative space with black. This book is for you to personalise as you please.

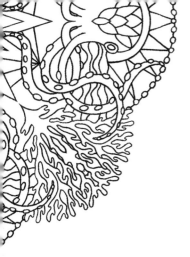

## GET STARTED!

There's no sequence to these mandalas, and you can get started anywhere you like in the book. Just pick one that looks right to you now – maybe one of the natural elements in the design speaks to you directly – pick up a pencil and relax into it. Stay aware of the shapes in the mandala, of the life it depicts, and the colours that you chose: appreciate the qualities of this moment, and acknowledge any underlying feelings, sensations or thoughts. You'll soon feel a benefit.

## MINDFUL COLOURING

Mindfulness is all about quieting your thoughts, freeing yourself from distraction, and appreciating the qualities of the present moment. Colouring in can be an excellent way to find this sense of awareness; if you focus on the pattern, and your chosen colours, you will soon find the worries and anxieties of modern life lulled and subdued. You'll emerge refreshed, calm and more alert than when you started; you could even arrive at the solution to a problem that's been vexing you.